doughwork

D1445478

doughwork

Salt dough for creative home decorating

Penny Boylan
Photography by Graham Rae

southwater

This edition is published by Southwater

Southwater is an imprint of
Anness Publishing Limited
Hermes House
88–89 Blackfriars Road
London SE1 8HA
tel. 020 7401 2077
fax 020 7633 9499

Distributed in the UK by
The Manning Partnership
251–253 London Road East
Batheaston
Bath BA1 7RL
tel. 01225 852 727
fax 01225 852 852

Distributed in the USA by
Anness Publishing Inc.
27 West 20th Street
Suite 504
New York
NY 10011
tel. 212 807 6739
fax 212 807 6813

Distributed in Australia by
Sandstone Publishing
Unit 1
360 Norton Street
Leichhardt
New South Wales 2040
tel. 02 9560 7888
fax 02 9560 7488

1 3 5 7 9 10 8 6 4 2

Publisher: Joanna Lorenz
Project Editor: Sarah Ainley
Designer: Bobbie Colgate Stone
Step Photography: Rodney Forte
Illustrator: Madeleine David

Previously published as *Inspirations: Salt Dough*

CONTENTS

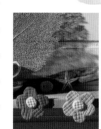

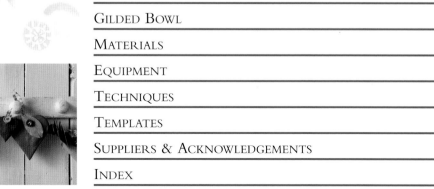

INTRODUCTION

THE USE OF SALT DOUGH for modelling has rocketed in popularity in recent years. Although it appears to be a recent craft, the origins of salt dough are with the ancient Egyptians, Romans and Greeks. I remember a local baker's shop always filling its window around harvest festival time with loaves made in the shape of wheatsheaves. Salt dough is a progression on from these loaves. The yeast is omitted and the salt content is increased to preserve the dough.

The beauty of salt dough is that it is so simple to use; it has tremendous tactile qualities and, made as it is from everyday ingredients, is both readily available and inexpensive. This makes salt dough the perfect creative material. In this book we update the traditional craft of salt dough with a wealth of items for your home. We show you how to make a lamp-base by moulding dough around a bowl and how to add embellishments to drawer handles and to tie-backs. As well as step-by-step instructions for each project, the book includes a comprehensive section to explain the skills and techniques involved in the craft, from baking the dough to repairing breaks and applying the decoration.

My favourite project shows you how to make flame curtain finials, gilded with gold leaf. The look is so professional, you would never realize that they are made from simple salt dough. I know that you will be inspired, as I have been, to open your kitchen cupboard, get out your flour and start mixing.

Deborah Barker

6

RUSTIC LAMP-BASE

Salt dough is strong enough to use for quite substantial objects: this spherical lamp-base is ingeniously moulded into two halves and cemented together with dough. The coiled relief decorations give the lamp-base the roughened texture of traditional pottery.

YOU WILL NEED
salt dough
rolling pin
2 small ovenproof bowls of the
same size, one preferably with
a foot
clear film (plastic wrap)
sharp knife
pair of compasses (compass)
modelling tools
baking sheet
white matt emulsion (latex)
paint
paintbrush
matt acrylic varnish
saw
small piece of 9 mm/½ in
medium density fibreboard
(MDF)
drill
bottle lamp fitting, flex and
plug
glue gun

1 Roll out two equal portions of the dough to make circles 5 mm/¼ in thick.

2 Cover the outside of each bowl with clear film (plastic wrap) to prevent the dough from sticking. Place one piece of dough on the bowl without a foot and press it down smoothly around the sides.

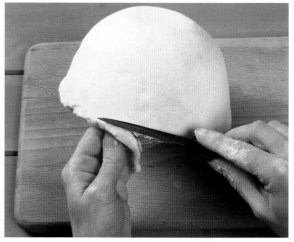

3 Trim the dough close to the edge of the bowl, using a sharp knife. This will form the lower part of the lamp-base.

4 Using the compasses (compass), mark a circle with an 8 cm/3 in diameter in the centre of the other piece of dough. Cut out, using a sharp knife.

5 Place the dough over the other bowl, placing the circular hole over the foot. Smooth down the sides and trim the edge, as before.

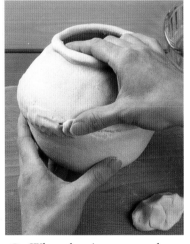

6 Roll a piece of dough into a sausage shape, then moisten the edge of the circular hole and press the sausage of dough on to it. Press the ends together to form the neck of the lamp-base.

7 Use a moistened modelling tool to smooth out the join. Transfer both bowls to a baking sheet and bake at 120°C/250°F/ Gas 1/2 for about 10 hours or until the dough is completely dry.

8 When the pieces are cool, pull them away from the moulds and glue the two halves together. Press small pieces of fresh dough along the moistened edges of the base to cover the join. Do this on the inside also. ▶

9 Smooth out the join with a moistened modelling tool. Return to the oven and bake for another 2 hours to allow the fresh dough to set a little.

10 Roll the remaining dough into long sausage shapes about as thick as your index finger. Then moisten the surface of the lamp-base and press on the sausage shapes gently in spiral patterns.

11 Smooth out the joins with a moistened modelling tool, then return to the oven and bake for a further 5 hours or until completely dry.

12 When the lamp-base is cool, apply three or four coats of white matt emulsion (latex) paint. Apply four coats of matt acrylic varnish, allowing it to dry between coats. Cut a small circular piece of MDF to fit the neck of the lamp-base and paint it white. Then drill a small hole in the base of the lamp, for the flex, and a larger hole in the centre of the MDF for the lamp fitting.

13 Glue the MDF piece into the neck of the lamp-base, using a glue gun.

SILVER LEAF DRAWER HANDLES

Stylish handles will instantly transform an ordinary chest of drawers. These elegant leaves with embossed veins are embellished with delicate silver leaf over a dark green base. The ordinary knobs that support them should have flat fronts so that the leaves can be securely glued on.

YOU WILL NEED
stiff cardboard, for template
pencil
scissors
rolling pin
salt dough
baking parchment
flour, for dusting
sharp knife
baking sheet
acrylic gesso
paintbrushes
dark green acrylic gouache paint
gold size
silver leaf
plain drawer knobs
strong wood glue or epoxy resin glue
gloss polyurethane varnish

1 Enlarge the template at the back of the book and copy it on to a piece of stiff cardboard. Cut out the central vein design, then cut round the leaf motif.

2 Roll out the dough on to baking parchment to a thickness of 8 mm/³⁄₈ in. Place the leaf template on the dough after dusting it lightly with flour to prevent it from sticking. Press the template into the dough so that the leaf veins protrude through the cut-away shape in the centre. Remove the template.

3 Cut away the excess dough with a sharp knife, smoothing the edges as you cut. When you have cut out a leaf for each handle, transfer the leaves carefully to a baking sheet lined with baking parchment and bake at 120°C/250°F/Gas 1/2 for 6 hours or until the leaves are completely dry.

4 Prime the cooled leaves with two coats of acrylic gesso. Then paint with two coats of dark green acrylic gouache paint. Allow to dry completely.

5 When the leaves are dry, paint them with gold size and leave them to stand until the surface is just tacky.

6 Apply the silver leaf to the fronts of the leaves, smoothing it down with a soft paintbrush and easing it into all the grooves of the leaf surface.

7 Glue the leaves on to plain, flat drawer knobs that can be screwed through the holes in the drawer fronts. Use strong wood glue or epoxy resin glue.

8 Apply silver leaf to the backs of the leaves, using a soft paintbrush. When dry, apply five coats of gloss polyurethane varnish to the fronts of the leaves.

LUSTRE BOTTLE STOPPERS

Use these glittering, iridescent stoppers in satisfying curly shapes to cork pretty bottles of
bath oils, salts and lotions. They are perfect for turning home-made potions into special gifts.

YOU WILL NEED
salt dough
rolling pin
aluminium foil
baking sheet
white matt emulsion (latex) paint
paintbrushes
acrylic paints in purple, lilac and cerise
pearlized paints in purple, lilac and cerise
matt polyurethane varnish
picture framer's wax gilt
gold jewellery wire
small pliers
epoxy resin glue
gold tassels

1 Divide the salt dough into golf ball-size portions. Roll out each ball of dough into an oval shape – use a rolling pin or just flatten it with your fingers.

2 Scrunch up strips of aluminium foil into oblong shapes to form the armatures for the stoppers. Place the foil on the flattened dough ball and roll up the edges to cover the foil completely.

3 Use your fingers to roll the dough to form a short sausage shape. The dough shape should be tapered at one end and blunt at the other.

▶

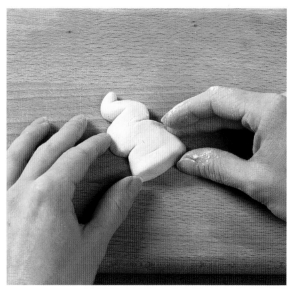

4 Bend the tapered sausage into an abstract curved
or wavy shape; the foil inside helps to hold the
shape. Place all the shapes on a baking sheet and bake
at 120°C/250°F/Gas 1/2 for 6 hours or until the
dough is completely dry.

5 When the stoppers are cool, prime them with
a coat of white matt emulsion (latex) paint, then
paint with acrylic paints. When dry, coat the stoppers
lightly with pearlized paints. Apply four coats of
matt polyurethane varnish, allowing each coat to
dry before applying the next.

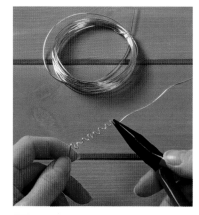

6 Rub picture framer's wax gilt
on to each of the stoppers
with your finger to accentuate
the raised curves.

7 Cut a length of gold
jewellery wire and, using
small pliers, bend the central
section into a zigzag long enough
to go around each of the stoppers.

8 Wind the gold wire around
the base of each bottle stopper, twist the ends together at
the back and snip off. Glue each
stopper to the top of a cork, using
epoxy resin glue. Add a gold tassel
to the neck of each bottle.

GILDED CURTAIN POLE FINIALS

These stately finials look like carved and gilded wood, and will enhance the most elegant
window treatment: it would be impossible to guess that they are made from so humble
a material as salt dough. The right-hand finial is shown in the photographs; make the two finials
at the same time, remembering to reverse the design for the left-hand side.

YOU WILL NEED
metal curtain pole
aluminium foil
salt dough
baking parchment
baking sheet
modelling tool
sharp knife
acrylic gesso
paintbrushes
red oxide acrylic gouache paint
gold size
Dutch metal leaf in gold
satin polyurethane varnish
strong glue

1 Cover the end of the metal curtain pole with aluminium foil and smooth the surface. Smooth a piece of dough over the foil-covered end.

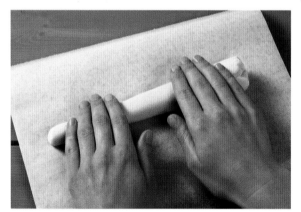

2 Roll a piece of dough into an elongated cone shape and place it on baking parchment on a baking sheet. Press the foil-covered end of the curtain pole into the cone shape, smoothing it with your fingers. Remove the curtain pole to leave just the foil.

3 Arrange the narrower end of the cone in a wave pattern. Make two more elongated cones, slightly smaller than the first, and arrange these on either side of the first cone, pressing them on to it where it meets the foil and shaping the ends.

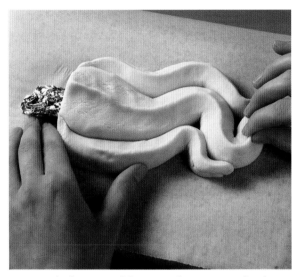

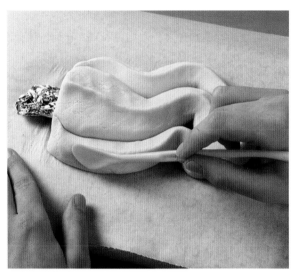

4 Pinch the tops of the cone shapes, to make sharp contours in the shape of the finials.

5 Use a modelling tool to smooth and ease the shapes until you are satisfied with the result.

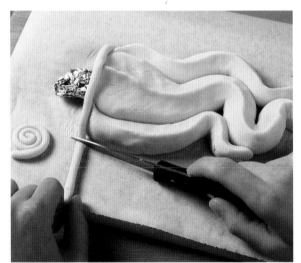

6 Roll out a thin sausage of dough, keeping it an even width throughout. Make this into a coil. Roll out another thin sausage of dough and use it to cover the end of the finial near where the pole will be inserted. Lay the coiled piece on top of this, sticking it down by moistening the surface. Bake in the oven at 120°C/250°F/Gas 1/2 for 6 hours, then turn the finials over and return to the oven for a further 4 hours or until completely dry.

7 Allow the dough to cool, then roll out a circle of dough about 10 mm/^{1}/$_2$ in thick to cover the back of each piece neatly. Dampen the back of the finial and place the dough in position. Return the finial to the oven for a further 4 hours or until it is completely dry. Repeat the procedure for the second finial.

▶

8 Prime the finials with two coats of acrylic gesso and allow them to dry thoroughly before painting with two coats of red oxide acrylic gouache. Allow to dry completely.

9 Paint the finials with a coat of gold size and leave until it is just tacky.

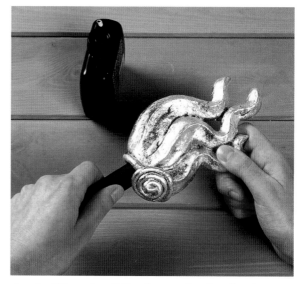

10 Gently apply the Dutch metal leaf, easing it over the contours and into the grooves with a soft dry paintbrush. Don't worry about cracks and splits as this adds to the antique effect.

11 When the gilding is completed, paint the finials with four coats of satin polyurethane varnish. Allow to dry between coats. Remove the aluminium foil and glue the finials firmly to the curtain pole, using a strong glue.

CANDLE SCONCE

Shimmering fragments of glass and mirror reflect the dancing candle flame in this simple but effective sconce in shades of blue and turquoise.

YOU WILL NEED

mosaic tiles in dark, mid- and light blue, at least 10 of each colour
tile clippers
15 cm/6 in mirror tile
glass-cutter
salt dough
baking parchment
baking sheet
rolling pin
paper, for template
pencil
scissors
sharp knife
candle, about 13 cm/5 in tall and 2 cm/³⁄₄ in in diameter
white matt emulsion (latex) paint
paintbrush
turquoise acrylic paint
gloss acrylic varnish
picture hanger
strong glue

1 Cut each mosaic tile in half using tile clippers. Cut a strip about 2.5 cm/1 in wide from the mirror tile, using a glass-cutter, and a small square of mirror for the front of the shelf.

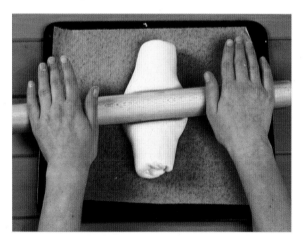

2 Roll the salt dough into a sausage shape, about 30 cm/12 in long, and lay it on a sheet of baking parchment on a baking sheet. Flatten the sausage with a rolling pin into a roughly oval shape, at least 2 cm/³⁄₄ in thick.

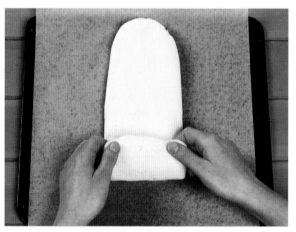

3 Scale up the template at the back of the book, transfer to paper and cut out. Fold up the bottom section of the dough oval to form the candle shelf, using the template as a guide to its position.

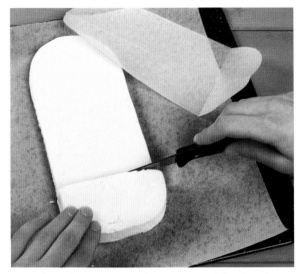

4 Place the paper template on top of the dough and cut around the top part of the shape with a sharp knife. Trim the top of the shelf, then replace the template and cut around it to make a rounded shape at the base of the sconce.

5 Use the candle to form a hole in the shelf by pressing it into the dough to a depth of about 2 cm/³/₄ in. Remove the candle.

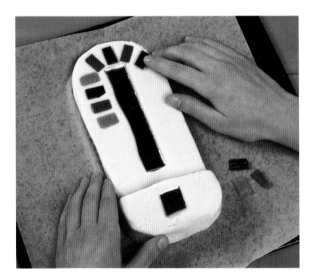

6 Apply the mirror strip centrally and arrange the mosaic tiles around it, alternating the colours. Press the pieces well into the dough by going over them gently with the rolling pin. Bake at 120°C/ 250°F/ Gas 1/2 for several hours or until the dough feels dry and hard to the touch.

7 When the baked dough has cooled, prime the sconce carefully with two coats of white matt emulsion (latex) paint.

▶

8 Leave to dry, then paint the sconce with a coat of turquoise acrylic paint.

9 Apply four coats of gloss acrylic varnish, allowing the varnish to dry between coats.

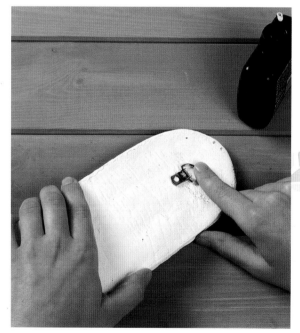

10 Finally, glue a picture hanger to the back of the sconce, using a strong glue.

TEA-TOWEL RACK

The design for this hook rack was inspired by the decorative relief mouldings made by Indian women around their door and window frames, using simple hand-rolled strips of clay applied in intricate patterns. Choose thin, soft paper when drawing the template: you must be able to pierce it easily with a pin without squashing the dough.

YOU WILL NEED

pencil	paintbrushes
thin paper	yellow acrylic gouache paint
scissors	matt acrylic varnish
rolling pin	medium-gauge galvanized
salt dough	wire
baking parchment	wire-cutters
flour, for dusting	pliers
sharp knife	piece of plywood or similar, not
large pin	more than 1 cm/^{1}/$_2$ in thick
2 baking sheets	saw
weights	panel pins (tacks)
acrylic gesso	hammer
	strong wood glue

1 Enlarge the template at the back of the book to 27 x 13 cm/10^1/$_2$ x 5 in and copy it on to a sheet of thin paper. Roll out the dough, on a sheet of baking parchment, to a thickness of 8 mm/^{3}/$_8$ in. Dust the dough very lightly with flour to prevent it sticking, place the template on it and cut out the rectangle with a sharp knife. With a pin, prick the details of the design through the template into the dough. Remove the template.

2 Break off small pieces of dough and roll them to make thin sausages about 5 mm/^{1}/$_4$ in in diameter. Use these strips to form the relief pattern, gently pressing them along the pricked lines after very lightly moistening the base. Do not make the dough too wet. Pinch the top of the relief moulding while easing each strip into place.

▶

3 Place the whole panel on its baking parchment on a baking sheet and bake at 120°C/250°F/Gas 1/2 for 8 to 10 hours. Watch the panel very carefully to see that it does not get too distorted. After several hours' baking, the relief mouldings will be quite strong, and you can weight the panel down with a second baking sheet, with heavy weights placed on top. Prime the panel with several coats of acrylic gesso.

4 When the panel of dough is dry, paint it with yellow acrylic gouache paint, then varnish it with four coats of matt acrylic varnish, allowing the varnish to dry between coats.

5 Make the hooks for the hanger by twisting galvanized wire around itself in short lengths using pliers, then bending it into a pleasing hook shape.

6 Make a wood backing board to mount the salt dough panel, cutting the wood slightly smaller than the baked panel. Paint the wood to match the panel if you wish. Attach hooks to the back, using panel pins (tacks) hammered in and bent over to secure the hooks. At the same time, make a loop of wire from which to hang the panel.

7 Glue the salt dough panel to the wood mount, using strong wood glue. Allow the glue to dry completely before hanging the panel.

"STONEWARE" CLOCK

The delicate "carving" around the face of this clock is easily achieved by embossing the soft dough with designs fashioned from small pieces of wire. Textured stone paint completes the effect.

YOU WILL NEED
rolling pin
salt dough
baking sheet
paper, for template
pencil
pair of compasses (compass)
scissors
sharp knife
wire-cutters
2 mm/⅛ in galvanized wire
pliers
white matt emulsion (latex) paint
paintbrush
stone-effect textured paint
matt polyurethane varnish
clock mechanism and hands

1 Roll out the salt dough in a circle to a thickness of 5 mm/¼ in. Transfer to a baking sheet. Draw and cut out a 24 cm/9½ in diameter circle of paper and place on the dough. Cut around the edge, using a sharp knife. Discard the excess dough.

2 Enlarge the embossing designs at the back of the book and copy them on plain paper. Cut two lengths of galvanized wire and use pliers to bend them to match the wavy pattern and the spiral. For the spiral, leave a "tail" of wire at both ends of the shape and bend them upwards to give you something to hold while embossing.

3 Emboss four spirals around the edge of the clock: at the hour, half-hour and quarter-hour points.

4 Make a hole in the centre of the face for the clock mechanism spindle, then emboss a series of wavy lines between each spiral. Bake at 120°C/250°F/Gas 1/2 for about 10 hours or until completely dry.

5 When the clock face is cool, prime it with white matt emulsion (latex) paint and leave to dry, then decorate with stone-effect textured paint. Apply four coats of matt polyurethane varnish, allowing each coat to dry before applying the next.

6 Insert the clock mechanism and hands, following the manufacturer's instructions.

30

INDIAN-STYLE DECORATIONS

These finely detailed ornaments are inspired by traditional Indian decorative motifs. Decorate them with the brightest possible paints and inks to evoke the vivid colours of an Indian festival.

YOU WILL NEED
thin cardboard, for templates
pencil
scissors
salt dough
rolling pin
baking parchment
flour, for dusting
sharp knife
toothpick and drinking straw
baking sheet
metal nail file
acrylic gesso
medium and fine paintbrushes
lime and dark green metallic inks
pink, orange and turquoise fluorescent acrylic paints
matt acrylic varnish
scrap of green foil crêpe paper
strong glue
selection of small beads and sequins

1 Enlarge the templates at the back of the book, transfer to cardboard and cut out. Roll out a small quantity of dough, on baking parchment, to a thickness of 5 mm/¼ in. Dust the templates with flour to prevent them from sticking. Place them on the dough and cut around the shapes with the knife.

2 For the flower design, cut out the holes in the petals with a sharp knife and emboss the central flower motif with the point of the knife.

3 Make the pricked patterns using a toothpick and a drinking straw. Make a hole in the top of each decoration for hanging.

4 Cut cardboard templates for the small shapes for the relief designs. Cut the shapes out of dough and stick them on the moistened surface of the decorations. Transfer the shapes, on the baking parchment, to a baking sheet and bake at 120°C/250°F/Gas 1/2 for 5 hours or until completely dry.

5 When the shapes have cooled, file the edges smooth and prime all the designs with two coats of acrylic gesso. For the flower design, paint with lime green metallic ink, then paint inside the petal cut-outs with darker green. Paint the fine details in bright pink fluorescent acrylic paint.

6 For the hand motif, paint all round the edges in bright pink fluorescent acrylic paint.

7 Paint the rest of the hand with bright orange acrylic paint. ▶

8 Add fine details in pink and bright turquoise, using the embossed areas as a guide. Paint all the decorations with four coats of matt acrylic varnish, leaving them to dry between coats.

9 To complete the hand, cut out a flower motif from a scrap of green foil crêpe paper and glue it down.

10 To complete the flower design, stick on small beads and sequins after painting the fine details in bright pink.

RELIEF-MOULDED PICTURE FRAME

It's not difficult to buy small Indian wooden textile-printing blocks such as the selection used to decorate this frame, but you could also use modelling tools to emboss the bird, flower and leaf designs.

YOU WILL NEED
thin cardboard, for template
pencil
scissors
salt dough
rolling pin
baking parchment
sharp knife
modelling tools
wooden printing blocks with bird, flower
and leaf designs
baking sheet
acrylic paints in terracotta and cream
paintbrushes
matt spray varnish
corrugated cardboard
glue gun or strong glue

1 Enlarge the template at the back of the book, transfer the outline to thin cardboard and cut out. Roll out the dough, on a sheet of baking parchment, to a thickness of 5 mm/$^{1}/_{4}$ in and cut around the template, using a sharp knife.

2 Smooth down the edges of the frame with a wet finger or modelling tool. Choose a long, narrow printing block and press it gently into the two sides of the frame.

3 Re-roll the remaining dough and stamp a bird shape into it. Cut carefully around the edges with the knife and smooth the edges, using a modelling tool.

4 Cut five large flowers out of the dough in the same way. Make sure that the dough is not too moist, or the blocks will become clogged.

5 Make five elongated leaf shapes and two smaller flower shapes. Moisten the back of each motif and position them around the frame, pressing them gently into the dough.

6 Using the rounded end of a modelling tool, press a row of small semicircles around the inner and outer edges of the frame. Fill in any remaining spaces with small stamped shapes.

7 Transfer the frame, still on the baking parchment, to a baking sheet and bake at 120°C/250°F/ Gas 1/2 for several hours or until completely hard. When cool, paint the frame with a thinnish wash of terracotta acrylic paint and allow to dry.

8 Using a dry bristle brush, lightly apply a layer of cream paint over the terracotta wash. Build it up in thin layers to emphasize the raised parts of the design, and be sure to allow the background colour to show through. ▶

9 When the paint is dry, spray the frame with a light coat of matt varnish on both sides.

10 Cut a rectangle of corrugated cardboard, 1 cm/¹/₂ in smaller all round than the frame, and glue it to the back, around the sides and lower edge. Cut a 7.5 x 15 cm/3 x 6 in piece of cardboard and make a 1 cm/¹/₂ in fold along one long edge. Trim the lower edge so that it slopes slightly upwards from the fold and glue the narrow folded strip to the back of the frame to form a stand.

DAISY SHELF BORDER

Attach a row of little flowers in fresh colours along the front of a plain shelf to turn it into a focal point. You could adapt this idea to other wooden furniture that needs cheering up, too.

YOU WILL NEED
stiff cardboard, for template
pencil
scissors
salt dough
rolling pin
baking parchment
sharp knife
flour, for dusting
baking sheet
acrylic gesso
paintbrush
acrylic gouache paints in pink and lime green
matt acrylic varnish
painted pine shelf
wood glue

1 Copy the daisy motif at the back of the book on to a piece of stiff cardboard and cut out. Using enough dough for one daisy at a time, roll the dough out to a thickness of 5 mm/¹/₄ in on a sheet of baking parchment. Place the template on the dough and press it down gently so that the centre of the daisy protrudes through the hole in the template. Cut around the shape with a sharp knife and gently pull away the excess dough.

2 Lift the template off very carefully; dust it lightly with flour between each use to prevent sticking. Tidy the rough edges with the flat of the knife. Make a criss-cross pattern all over the daisy with the knife blade. Repeat to make as many daisies as you need for the length of your shelf.

3 Transfer the daisies, still on baking parchment, to a baking sheet and bake at 120°C/250°F/ Gas 1/2 for about 6 hours or until completely hard. Allow to cool, then prime the daisies with two coats of acrylic gesso. Allow to dry.

▶

4 Paint the daisies with pink and lime green acrylic gouache, leaving the centres white. Allow the daisies to dry completely.

5 Finish the daisies with two to three coats of matt acrylic varnish. Allow the varnish to dry between coats.

6 Stick the motifs on to the edge of the painted shelf, using wood glue.

These painted daisies will add a unique freshness to any shelf edge or piece of furniture, indoors or out.

INDIAN GODDESS WALL PLAQUE

This impressive plaque is built up over a mould to give depth and solidity, and the three-dimensional effect is completed with the applied features. The paint effect makes it look exactly like a terracotta relief sculpture.

YOU WILL NEED

paper, for template	toothpick
pencil	terracotta matt emulsion (latex)
scissors	paint
salt dough	paintbrushes
rolling pin	terracotta-effect textured paint
sharp knife	acrylic paints in black and gold
small saucer	matt polyurethane varnish
aluminium foil	gold jewellery wire
baking sheet	picture hanger
modelling tool	strong glue

1 Enlarge the plaque template at the back of the book, copy the outline and features on to a sheet of paper and cut out. Roll out the dough to a thickness of 5 mm/¼ in. Cut around the outline of the template, using a sharp knife.

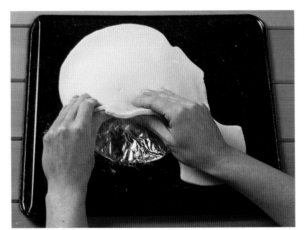

2 Cover the convex side of the saucer with aluminium foil, then place the saucer on a baking sheet and carefully lift the dough shape and place it on top of the saucer.

3 Press the edges of the shape smooth, using your fingers then, using a modelling tool, draw the hairline, eyes, eyebrows, nose and chin. Use the template as a guide to their positions.

▶

43

4 Cut out the shapes for the headdress, eyes, mouth and nose from the paper template. Roll out some more dough to a thickness of 5 mm/ ¹/₄ in and cut out all the shapes with a sharp knife. Moisten the surface of the plaque and stick the shapes in place.

5 Use a moistened modelling tool to press in line details on the headdress, eyes and mouth. Pierce small holes through the ear lobes, using a toothpick.

6 Roll small quantities of dough into thin tapered sausages and add eyebrows and the border of the headdress. Use small balls of dough to make the necklace and forehead decoration. Smooth out the joins with a moistened modelling tool. Bake the plaque at 120°C/250°F/Gas 1/2 for several hours or until completely dry.

7 When the plaque is cool, apply an undercoat of terracotta matt emulsion (latex) paint, then paint on a base coat of terracotta-effect textured paint. Highlight the features and details using acrylic paints. Apply four coats of matt varnish, allowing each coat to dry before applying the next. Add wire loops for the ear lobes, and glue a picture hanger to the back.

JEWELLED MIRROR FRAME

*This extravagantly jewelled frame is full of light and organic movement and looks like some
fabulous marine treasure. Small fragments of mirror are set into the frame: be very careful when
smashing a mirror to make these; wrap it in newspaper before hitting it with a hammer.*

YOU WILL NEED
thin cardboard, for template
pencil
scissors
rolling pin
salt dough
baking parchment
sharp knife
modelling tools
flower-shaped wooden printing block
glass nuggets
fragments of shattered mirror
acrylic paints in gold, blue, green and yellow
paintbrushes
clear nail varnish
mirror
glue gun or strong glue
picture hanger

1 Enlarge the template at the back of the book,
transfer the outline to thin cardboard and cut
out. Roll out the dough to a thickness of 5 mm/
¼ in on a sheet of baking parchment and use the
template to cut out the frame with a sharp knife.

2 Smooth and curve the edges of the dough with
a modelling tool.

3 Use a modelling tool to emboss coiled shapes in
the rounded points of the frame.

4 Make the "cabuchon" jewel settings by pressing a wooden printing block into the dough to form a flower-shaped surround. (Alternatively, you could achieve the same effect using a modelling tool.) Push a glass nugget firmly into the centre of each flower. Roll small pieces of dough into balls about 4 mm/¹⁄₆ in across and arrange these in a ring around each nugget.

5 Press other glass nuggets directly into the dough. Space the nuggets evenly between the flowers, around the edge of the frame, leaving enough space for the mirror pieces.

6 Embed the mirror fragments randomly in any remaining spaces around the frame. Use a modelling tool to push them into place to avoid cutting your fingers.

7 Bake in the oven at 120°C/250°F/Gas 1/2 for several hours, until the dough is completely dry and hard. Paint the background with gold paint.

▶

8 Paint the jewel settings and their surrounds in blue, green and yellow acylic paints.

9 When the paint is dry, varnish the coloured areas with a coat of clear nail varnish.

10 Glue the mirror in place, using a glue gun or strong glue, and glue a picture hanger to the back of the frame.

Vary the colour scheme of the beads and baubles, according to the style you wish to achieve.

COILED CANDLESTICKS

Chunky coils of dough built up around a chicken-wire frame make weighty candlesticks,
full of character. Paint the candlesticks the same colour to make a stunning table centrepiece.

YOU WILL NEED
wire-cutters
chicken wire
1.2 mm galvanized wire
0.3 mm galvanized wire
salt dough
modelling tool
baking sheet
white matt emulsion (latex) paint
paintbrush
blue acrylic paint
matt polyurethane varnish

1 Using wire-cutters, cut a 15 x 20 cm/6 x 8 in rectangle of chicken wire.

2 Bend the chicken wire to form a cylinder, twisting the ends together at the seam.

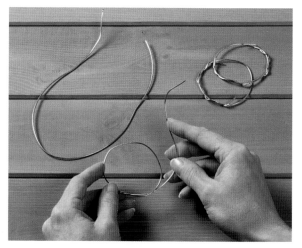

3 Cut two lengths of the thicker galvanized wire and bend to form rings, one about 6 cm/2½ in in diameter for the base, and the other 5 cm/2 in in diameter for the top of the candlestick.

50

4 Place one ring over the top of the cylinder and bend the ends of the chicken wire over to hold it in place.

5 Take a length of thinner wire and "oversew" the ring around the edge of the armature. Attach the other ring at the base in the same way.

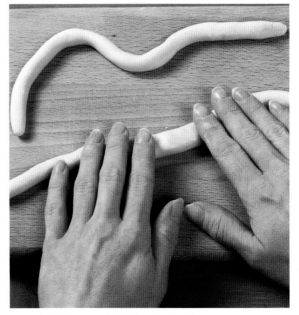

6 Squeeze the cylinder to make it slightly narrower in the centre.

7 Roll pieces of salt dough into long sausage shapes, about as thick as your index finger. ▶

8 Beginning at the base of the candlestick, wrap the sausages around in a spiral, pressing the dough lightly on to the chicken-wire base.

9 Moisten the end of a modelling tool and smooth out the joins between the coils of dough. Transfer the candlestick to a baking sheet and bake at 120°C/250°F/Gas 1/2 for about 10 hours or until completely dry.

10 When the baked candlestick is cool, prime with a coat of white matt emulsion (latex) paint, then colour with blue acrylic paint. Apply four coats of matt polyurethane varnish, allowing each coat to dry before applying the next.

TRADITIONAL WHEATSHEAF

The wonderful colour of baked dough lends itself beautifully to this classic design, reminiscent of the traditional harvest loaf, which is given a new twist with a binding of natural raffia.

YOU WILL NEED
thin cardboard, for template
pencil
scissors
salt dough
rolling pin
baking parchment
sharp knife
modelling tools
galvanized wire, for hanging
baking sheet
matt acrylic varnish
paintbrush
natural raffia

1 Enlarge the template at the back of the book to a height of 25 cm/10 in, transfer the outline to thin cardboard and cut out. Roll out half the dough on a sheet of baking parchment to a thickness of 5 mm/¼ in and cut out the background shape, using a sharp knife.

2 Roll small lumps of the remaining dough into 10 cm/4 in sausages, about 4 mm/¹⁄₆ in in diameter.

3 Moisten the background and glue on the stalks. Leave a gap of about 2 cm/¾ in for the raffia tie, then add another section of stalks.

4 To mould the ears of corn, start by making a flat pad of dough about 4 x 1 cm/1½ x ½ in.

5 Use a flat-ended modelling tool to press a chevron pattern along the centre of the ear.

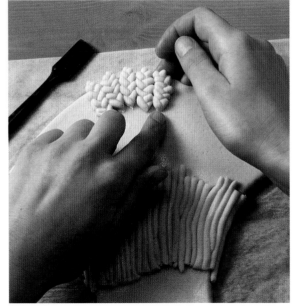

6 Trim away the end of each section of the ear and smooth into a curve. Repeat to make enough ears to fill the top row.

7 Moisten the top of the background and place a line of ears around the outer edge.

▶

8 Bend a piece of galvanized wire into a loop. Push it into the back of the wheatsheaf, for hanging.

9 Make more ears to fill another two rows, then lift the sheaf, on the baking parchment, on to a baking sheet and bake at 150°C/300°F/Gas 2 until lightly coloured. Turn the oven down and continue to bake until dry and hard.

10 When cool, varnish with four coats of matt acrylic varnish on both sides, leaving the varnish to dry between coats.

11 Cut a bundle of natural raffia to a length of 50 cm/20 in and tie in a reef knot around the centre of the wheatsheaf. Trim the ends.

MEXICAN BOWL

You could fill this striking spotty bowl with fruit, nuts or sweets, but you might prefer to display it empty, to enjoy its vibrant colours and exciting texture.

YOU WILL NEED
salt dough
rolling pin
ovenproof metal or ceramic bowl
cooking oil
sharp knife
small circular pastry or aspic cutter, or
metal screw top from a miniature bottle
white matt emulsion (latex) paint
paintbrush
acrylic paints in bright pink,
cadmium orange and burnt umber
toothbrush
gloss acrylic varnish

1 Roll out the salt dough to a thickness of about 8 mm/³⁄₈ in. Roll into a circle approximately 5 cm/2 in larger all round than the ovenproof bowl.

2 Oil the ovenproof bowl. Lay the dough over the bowl and press down gently. Trim the edges with a sharp knife.

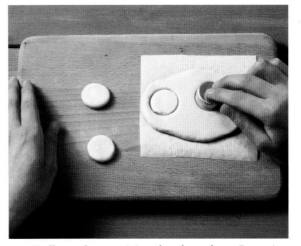

3 Roll out the remaining dough to about 5 mm/¹⁄₄ in and cut into circles using a small pastry cutter or bottle top. (If the salt dough becomes stuck in the bottle top, flick it out, using the point of a sharp knife.) ▶

4 Arrange the disks evenly over the salt dough bowl and gently press them into the surface of the dough.

5 Bake at 120°C/250°F/Gas 1/2 for about 7 hours or until hard and dry. Remove the mould. When the bowl has cooled, prime it with a coat of white matt emulsion (latex) paint. Leave to dry.

6 Using acrylic paint, colour the spots cadmium orange and the background bright pink. Paint the underside of the bowl pink.

7 Dilute some burnt umber acrylic paint and use an old toothbrush to splatter it over the bowl, flicking the bristles with your thumb. Varnish the bowl with four coats of gloss acrylic varnish.

BEADED CURTAIN TIE-BACKS

These stark white dough beads look like bleached pebbles collected on the beach, and add
the perfect finishing touch to unfussy curtains in plain natural fabrics.

YOU WILL NEED
salt dough
toothpick
baking sheet
baking parchment
acrylic gesso
paintbrush
natural raffia
scissors
darning needle

1 Make beads by breaking off pieces of dough and rolling them into balls. Use different amounts of dough to vary the size of the beads. Flatten some of the balls and mark indentations with a toothpick. Gently press the stick into the dough around some of the rounded beads, but leave others completely plain.

2 Make a hole through each bead with a toothpick, making sure the stick goes right through and the hole is not too small, otherwise it may close up during baking. Then place the beads on a baking sheet lined with baking parchment, ready for baking.

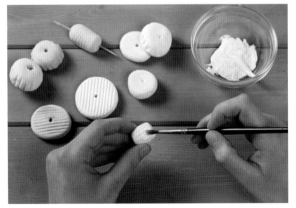

3 Bake at 120°C/250°F/Gas 1/2 for several hours or until completely dry. Prime with white acrylic gesso. If you find it helpful, push a toothpick through the hole to keep your hands clean while painting. Give each bead several coats of gesso. Allow to dry.

▶

4 Make three tassels from even lengths of natural raffia. Each length of raffia should have a loop at the top, for hanging. Trim the raffia tassels, as necessary, to neaten the ends.

5 Thread a darning needle with two to three strands of raffia long enough to go round the curtain and tie at the back. Thread the tassels on to the foundation raffia and tie in place, then add the painted beads until the tieback is the right size for the curtain.

6 Finish the tassels off by threading a few beads on to them at random.

ANIMAL ACROBAT BOOKENDS

Inspired by South American folk art, these delightful animals will be popular with children and adults alike. Use aluminium foil as an armature, to provide the basic animal shape.

YOU WILL NEED

pencil

ruler

10 cm x 12 mm/4 x ½ in pine

wood saw

fine sandpaper

wood glue

hammer

panel pins (tacks)

white matt emulsion (latex)

paint

paintbrushes

quick-drying gloss enamel paint in red, blue and yellow

aluminium foil

salt dough

modelling tool

baking sheet

bradawl

wooden skewer

gloss polyurethane varnish

strong glue

1 Use a pencil and ruler to draw a shape for the bookends on pieces of wood and cut the wood to size. Smooth any rough edges with fine sandpaper.

2 Glue the vertical sections at right angles to the bases. When the glue is dry, hammer in a few panel pins to hold the joints firm. Prime the wood with a coat of white matt emulsion (latex) paint.

3 When the emulsion is dry, paint the bookends in bright red enamel paint. Use a blue paint for the edges and finish with spots or stripes in yellow. Leave to dry.

4 Tear aluminium foil into strips and crumple it up to form rough head and body shapes for the elephants and llamas. (The little bird is made from dough only.)

5 Scrunch up more strips of foil to make four legs for each animal. Make each pair of animals at the same time to ensure that they match.

6 Wrap more pieces of foil around each armature to make a smoother shape.

7 Using small pieces of dough, cover the foil armature completely, smoothing out any irregularities with your fingers.

8 Use more dough to add features such as ears and tails. Smooth out the joins with a moistened modelling tool. Model the two birds in dough. Transfer all the animals to a baking sheet and bake in the oven at 120°C/250°F/Gas 1/2 for about 7 hours or until completely dry.

9 Use a bradawl to pierce a hole in the underside of each bird and glue in a short piece of wooden skewer: this acts as a handle when painting and as a stand when assembling the bookends. Prime each animal with a coat of white matt emulsion paint, then decorate with enamel paints. When dry, apply four coats of gloss polyurethane varnish, allowing each coat to dry before applying the next.

10 Using strong glue, glue an elephant by its feet to each bookend base. Pierce a hole with the bradawl in the back of each llama and attach the bird.

11 Finally, glue the llamas on to the backs of the elephants, using strong glue.

COUNTRY HEARTS GARLAND

For country-style festivities make this lovely garland using a favourite folk-art motif, the heart, painted in traditional shades. Use scraps of homespun fabrics to trim the hearts, in keeping with the country feel – try dipping cotton ticking in tea to give it an aged look.

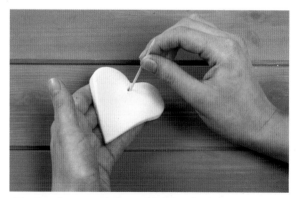

YOU WILL NEED

salt dough	soft pencil
rolling pin	acrylic gouache paints in
baking parchment	yellow, slate blue, oxide red
heart-shaped cookie cutters	matt acrylic varnish
sharp knife	string
toothpick	buttons
baking sheet	scraps of cotton fabrics
metal nail file or sandpaper	large darning needle
acrylic gesso	decorative twine
medium and fine paintbrushes	dried bay leaves

1 Roll out a piece of salt dough to a thickness of 5 mm/¼ in on a sheet of baking parchment. Using different sizes of cutter, press the cutters firmly into the dough. It is better to cut not more than two hearts at the same time, as removing the excess dough can cause distortion.

2 Gently remove the excess dough and round the edges of the heart with your fingers. Smooth any rough edges with a sharp knife. Make a hole in the top of the heart with a toothpick, making sure it goes right through and is big enough not to close up during baking.

3 Lift the hearts on to a baking sheet lined with baking parchment and bake in the oven at 120°C/250°F/Gas 1/2 for at least 5–6 hours, turning them over halfway through the cooking time.

4 When the dough is completely dry and cool, smooth out any rough edges with a nail file or some fine sandpaper.

5 Prime the hearts with two coats of acrylic gesso and leave to dry.

6 Trace the small motifs on to a sheet of baking parchment, using a soft pencil. Transfer the designs by placing the tracings pencil side down on the primed heart shapes and drawing over the motifs again.

7 Paint the small motifs with acrylic gouache in yellow ochre, slate blue and oxide red.

▶

8 Paint both sides of each heart in one of the three colours. When the paint is completely dry, protect with matt acrylic varnish. Allow to dry.

9 Thread a length of string through the hole in the top of each heart, using a darning needle. Tie on buttons and scraps of homespun cotton fabrics.

10 Thread the hearts on to a length of decorative twine, adding more buttons, dried bay leaves and strips of fabrics to complete the garland. Some of the hearts can be used as gift tags for presents.

BERRY LEAF NAPKIN RINGS

Exquisite moulded ornaments put the ultimate finishing touch to a special table setting.
To tie the napkins, use lustrous silk taffeta ribbon that will match the iridescent colours
of the leaves. Ready-made moulds are available from specialist cake-decorating suppliers.

YOU WILL NEED

rolling pin	baking sheet
salt dough	wood glue
pastry brush	acrylic gesso
ready-made moulds for leaves	paintbrushes
and small flowers	gold craft paint
cooking oil	watercolour inks in bright
baking parchment	green and bright pink
sharp knife	iridescent acrylic paint
aluminium foil	satin acrylic varnish
	decorative wire-edged ribbon

1 Roll out a small piece of dough to a thickness of 8 mm/³/₈ in. Brush the leaf mould with a thin coat of cooking oil.

2 Press the dough into the mould, making sure it reaches into all the fine details and grooves.

3 Gently ease the dough out of the mould and place it on a sheet of baking parchment. Cut away the excess dough neatly with a sharp knife, rounding the edges with the flat of the knife. Repeat to make as many leaves as you need.

4 Make an armature for the loop from a small rectangle of aluminium foil, folded over and over into a firm strip. Roll a narrow sausage of dough and lay this over the loop armature, trimming away the excess dough and smoothing the shape with your fingers. Make a loop for each leaf.

5 Gently lift the leaves on to a baking sheet lined with baking parchment, placing two or three small flattened balls of dough under each leaf shape, to give it an undulating profile.

6 Now repeat steps 1 to 5, using the flower mould, making a flower for each leaf, plus a few spares on which to experiment with colours. Bake all the leaves, loops and flowers at 120°C/250°F/Gas 1/2 for 6 hours or until completely dry.

7 When everything is cool, stick a loop to the back of each leaf, using wood glue.

8 Prime the leaves and flowers with two coats of acrylic gesso. Allow to dry, then paint with gold craft paint. Use a yellowish gold colour.

9 Paint the leaves with bright green watercolour ink and the flowers with bright pink watercolour ink. Allow to dry, then paint leaves and flowers with a thin coat of iridescent acrylic paint. Varnish with four coats of satin acrylic varnish. Allow to dry.

10 When the paints have dried completely, glue a flower to each leaf, using wood glue.

11 Thread co-ordinating wire-edged ribbon through the loop under each leaf and tie around a table napkin, making a bow at the front.

GILDED BOWL

Light and shade play over the embossed surface of this sumptuous bowl. The texture is easily achieved by pressing a strip of corrugated cardboard into the soft dough.

YOU WILL NEED
cooking oil
ovenproof bowl
pastry brush
baking sheet
baking parchment
salt dough
rolling pin
sharp knife
strip of fine corrugated cardboard
fine sandpaper
acrylic gesso
paintbrushes
acrylic gouache paint in red oxide and bright pink
gold size
Dutch metal leaf in gold
matt polyurethane varnish

1 Oil the ovenproof bowl you are using as a mould and invert it on to a baking sheet lined with baking parchment. Roll out the dough to a thickness of 8 mm/³⁄₈ in and large enough to cover the bowl. Make a slightly drier dough than usual to avoid it stretching and tearing.

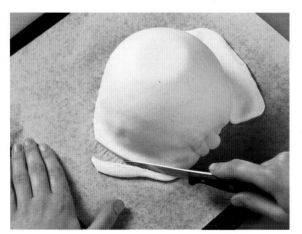

2 Lift the dough carefully on to the bowl and smooth it over the sides without stretching it. Cut away the excess dough with a sharp knife.

3 Turn the bowl over and trim the edge of the dough level with the bowl, using a sharp knife. Invert the bowl again.

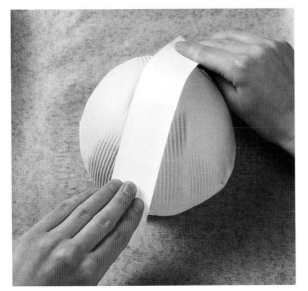

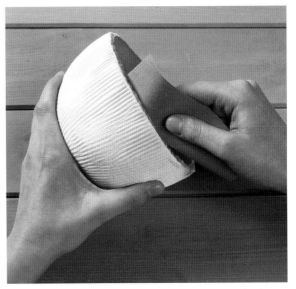

4 Using a strip of fine corrugated cardboard, gently emboss the sides of the bowl with a series of ridges.

5 Bake the bowl at 120°C/250°F/Gas 1/2 for 6 hours, then remove the mould and return the salt dough bowl to the oven, right side up, to dry the inside. When cool, smooth the edges with fine sandpaper.

6 Prime the bowl with three coats of acrylic gesso and allow to dry. Paint the outside of the bowl with red oxide acrylic paint, using two coats if necessary, to cover the white gesso.

7 Paint a thin layer of gold size over the red oxide colour and leave it to dry until the surface is just tacky.

▶

8 Apply sheets of Dutch metal leaf, gently pressing it into the textured ridges, using a clean soft paintbrush. Don't worry about splits and cracks as these add to the antique effect of the gilding.

9 Paint the inside of the bowl and the top edge with bright pink acrylic gouache, applying several coats to build up a good depth of colour.

10 Varnish the bowl inside and out with four or five coats of matt polyurethane varnish.

MATERIALS

ACRYLIC GESSO (1) This is invaluable for sealing the dough prior to decorating. It also adds strength to the dough and can mask fine cracks. Wash brushes well after using gesso, or they will harden.

ACRYLIC VARNISH (2) Acrylic varnish is available in matt, satin and gloss finishes. Use several coats to strengthen and protect the baked dough, and to make it wipeable for cleaning.

ALUMINIUM FOIL (3) Protects delicate items so they do not burn during baking. Also used for armatures.

BAKING PARCHMENT (4) Use a non-stick paper as used for home baking.

CHICKEN WIRE (5) This is used to form armatures.

COOKING OIL (6) Brush on to moulds so that the dough releases easily, after baking.

GLUE (7) Strong woodworking glue is used to attach sections of baked dough and to repair accidents.

GOLD AND SILVER LEAF (8) Although these are expensive, a little goes a long way. Buy the cheaper Dutch metal leaf for these projects.

GOLD SIZE (9) Use to apply metal leaf, when gilding.

MOSAIC TILES (10) Available in a range of colours.

PAINTS (11) Almost any paint can be used to decorate salt dough. Prime the dough with gesso before painting to provide a good surface to work on.

PLAIN FLOUR (12) Use ordinary household flour to make the dough. Self-raising flour is not suitable.

PAPER AND CARDBOARD (13) Cut templates from paper or cardboard. Use thin paper or baking parchment if you need to transfer fine details of the design.

POLYURETHANE VARNISH (14) As a varnish, it has a yellowing effect and is more suitable for use on gilded items. It is also a cheaper alternative to gold size for applying metal leaf when gilding.

RAFFIA (15) Use as an interesting alternative to string.

SALT (16) Acts as a preservative and also deters children from eating the dough when modelling with it.

TURPENTINE (17) Use to clean paintbrushes after use.

WIRE AND PICTURE HANGERS (18) For hanging the piece. Embed into the back of the unbaked dough.

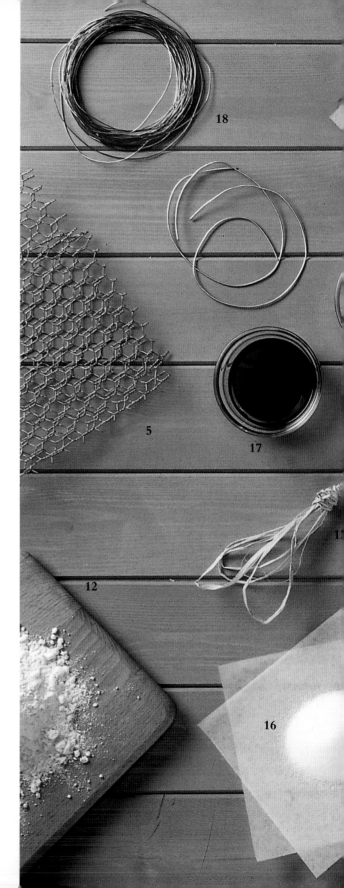

EQUIPMENT

BAKING SHEET (1) A sturdy baking sheet should never buckle during the drying-out process.

CHOPPING (CUTTING) BOARD (2) Use to protect the work surface if cutting with a sharp knife. Line with baking parchment to work on your project; lift dough and parchment together to transfer to a baking tray.

CLAY MODELLING TOOL (3) Use for shaping and smoothing awkward shapes.

CORRUGATED CARDBOARD (4) Use to emboss patterns on to the unbaked pieces of dough.

GLUE GUN (5) Use to assemble sections of models and to attach decorations such as beads or mirrors.

METAL RULER (6) Use when drawing templates.

MIXING BOWLS (7) Use a large bowl to mix the ingredients and to knead the dough.

MOULDS AND COOKIE CUTTERS (8) There are many moulds for cookery to be found in catering shops. Look out for antique chocolate and small jelly moulds for instant effects.

MUG OR CUP (9) Always use the same mug or cup for measuring ingredients in the same proportions.

PAINTBRUSHES (10) Build up a collection of sizes. Always keep brushes clean and store them upright.

PASTRY BRUSH (11) Dip into cooking oil and lightly grease a mould before covering with salt dough.

PLIERS (12) Use to protect your hands when working with wire and to shape armatures in chicken wire.

ROLLING PIN (13) Use for rolling out areas of dough.

SANDPAPER AND NAIL FILE (14) Essential for smoothing burrs and rough edges on the baked dough.

SCISSORS (15) Use to cut out templates.

SHARP KNIFE (16) Use a small kitchen knife to cut the dough around templates.

TILES (17) Use to roll out dough at an even height.

TILE CUTTERS (18) Use to cut mosaic tiles to size, or to make your own pieces of mirror or broken ceramics.

TOOTHPICKS (19) Use for making decorative holes in the salt dough. A darning needle can also be used.

WOODEN SPOON (20) Mix the ingredients with a wooden spoon before kneading the dough.

TECHNIQUES

The most important thing to remember with salt dough is that the dough should be allowed to dry out slowly. Do not be tempted to increase the heat and rush the baking the time.

MAKING DOUGH

1 Measure out 2 cups of plain flour, 1 cup of salt and 1 scant cup of tepid water, using the same cup or mug for each ingredient. Combine the flour and salt in a large mixing bowl, adding half the water at first. Mix the ingredients with a wooden spoon, gradually adding more water, until you have a firm dough that is not too wet. If the dough becomes too sticky, add more flour and continue to mix until the dough becomes firm. Flour your hands to complete the mixing on a work surface.

2 It is important to knead the dough thoroughly for at least 10 minutes to achieve an elastic consistency. The dough can be used immediately, but is best left to rest at room temperture for about 30 minutes in a plastic bag. Unused dough can be stored in the fridge for up to three days. If the dough becomes excessively wet and sticky during storage, add more flour and knead very thoroughly until it becomes smooth and elastic again. You will soon become used to the correct consistency needed for a pliable dough. Old or wet dough is too stretchy and does not keep its shape well.

ROLLING OUT DOUGH

1 Roll out salt dough on to a flat surface lined with baking parchment or directly on to a work surface dusted with flour. If the rolling pin becomes sticky, dust it very lightly with plain flour. The baking parchment and rolled-out dough can be lifted together, with the minimum of disturbance, on to the baking sheet, ready for drying in the oven.

2 When rolling out flat items of dough, it is useful to place two ceramic tiles on either side of the dough for the rolling pin to rest against. The tiles act as a guide for making the dough an even depth.

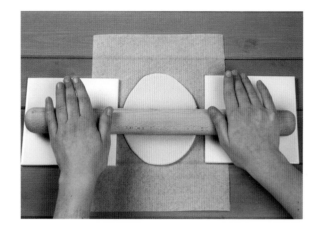

CUTTING AROUND A TEMPLATE

1 A template can be made from paper or cardboard, or from baking parchment, which has the advantage of being transparent. Place the template on to the rolled-out dough and cut around it, using a small, sharp knife. Remove the excess dough, then work around the image, trimming away rough edges. Pat the edges of the image with your finger or the flat part of the knife to create a rounded edge.

2 Details on the image can be transferred to the dough by replacing the template and pricking through the design with a pin. Remove the template to reveal the design. Enhance the image on the dough by joining the dots with a toothpick or with the point of a sharp knife.

EMBOSSING AND EMBEDDING

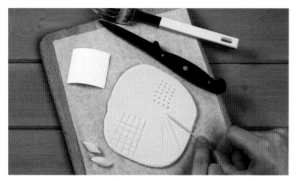

1 The surface of the dough can be decorated with a wide variety of textures. Experiment on spare pieces of dough, using different implements, to create embossed patterns until you have found a texture suitable for the object you are making. Some ideas for modelling implements might include a small knife, a fork, toothpicks, corrugated cardboard, a comb and a pair of scissors to snip the edges. Look out for ready-made embossing tools, such as those used for cake decorating, and even printing blocks for textiles.

2 Various materials can be embedded in the dough to create a decorative effect. Shells, glass beads, mosaic tiles and broken china can be pressed into the dough; smooth around the edge of the object with a moistened finger. If you plan to hang the item when it is finished, press a small loop of wire into the dough, at the back of the object, before baking.

USING READY-MADE MOULDS

1 Look out for ready-made moulds and cutters used for cake decorating in cookery shops and children's toyshops. Ovenproof bowls and plates also make successful moulds. Always coat the mould with a layer of cooking oil before applying the dough, so that the dough will release easily once baked. Roll out the dough to a thickness of 8 mm/⅜ in, making sure it is large enough to cover the mould.

2 Lift the rolled dough carefully into place; it must not be too moist or it will stretch and make holes, so use a drier mixture than usual. Smooth the dough around the mould, taking care not to leave indentations from your fingers.

WORKING OVER AN ARMATURE

1 Cardboard can be used for making armatures, to provide the structure of the object. (Anything that remains ovenproof at low temperatures can also be used.) Cover with aluminium baking foil, then gently spread the salt dough around the armature.

2 Larger objects require a chicken wire armature to provide the structure. Use pliers to shape the wire armature, then cover it with salt dough. Large models can be part-baked and the armature turned around, as other sections of dough are added.

BAKING THE DOUGH

1 Bake the dough items on a domestic baking sheet lined with non-stick baking parchment, placed on a low shelf in the oven. Several items can be baked at the same time; rotate the shelf positions for each baking sheet to achieve even results. It is important to bake salt dough slowly, at a low temperature (120°C/250°F/Gas 1/2) to avoid distortion, cracking and discolouring. When the given baking time has been reached, switch off the oven, leavng the baked item inside to cool, to complete the drying out process. All baking times for the projects are approximate.

2 Items that are to remain a natural colour can be baked at a slightly higher temperature, to give colour. Bake at 150°C/300°F/Gas 2, checking the piece often. When the desired colour has been reached, turn down the oven and place the object on the lowest shelf to continue drying out.

3 Items can also be part-baked and returned to the oven to be finished later on. This is a useful technique for three-dimensional items. Build up the object in sections; part-bake the first section for at least three hours, then add a further section and return the whole thing to the oven. Repeat as many times as is necessary to build up the shape. To stick raw salt dough to part-baked dough, moisten with water, apply the salt dough and press together gently.

4 Large flat pieces of dough can be weighted down to keep them flat, after baking in the oven for at least three hours. Place an ovenproof plate on top of the item, making sure the weight is evenly distributed, and return to the oven to complete the baking time.

REPAIRS

1 Repair cracks that appear during baking by mixing some salt dough to a paste with water and filling the fissure before returning it to the oven.

2 Repair broken work that is already baked with strong wood glue. Wipe away the excess glue with a tissue and allow to dry before decorating.

SMOOTHING EDGES

3 Repairs to painted work can also be made with strong wood glue. Wipe away the excess glue with a tissue and allow to dry completely.

1 Rough edges and burrs can be smoothed out easily with a metal nail file or fine sandpaper.

DECORATING

1 Prepare salt dough for decorating by priming first with acrylic gesso. This gives extra strength to the dough and provides a good surface for painting. Ordinary household emulsion (latex) paint can also be used as a primer. Give each piece of dough several coats, but do not cover fine details too thickly.

2 When the primer is competely dry the model can be painted. A wide variety of paints can be used on salt dough: acrylic gouache is especially good, but coloured inks, metallic paints and sprays can all be used effectively.

3 Always varnish the model after painting to protect the surface from dust and moisture. (It is important to remember that salt dough cannot be used for items that hold water.) Allow paint to dry for at least 6 hours, as the item must be completely dry before varnishing. Apply at least 4 coats of varnish, allowing each coat to dry before applying the next. The type of varnish you use depends on personal preference; choose from gloss, matt or satin finish polyurethane varnish, available from hardware stores. Less economical but very good are artist-quality acrylic varnishes in a wide variety of finishes. Polyurethane varnishes tend to be yellowish in colour: this is acceptable over gold leaf and certain colours but may not be suitable for more subtly coloured items.

TEMPLATES

Indian-style Decorations,
pp32–5

"STONEWARE" CLOCK,
PP29–31

DAISY SHELF BORDER, PP40–4

COUNTRY HEARTS GARLAND, PP68–71

CANDLE SCONCE, PP22–5

SILVER LEAF DRAWER HANDLES,
PP12–14

RELIEF-MOULDED PICTURE FRAME,
PP36–9

JEWELLED MIRROR FRAME,
PP46–9